Copyright © 2025 Frederick Barnes. All rights reserved. ISBN: 978-1-0670695-3-7 No part of this publication may be reproduced, distributed, or transmitted in any form or by any means, including photocopying, recording, or other electronic or mechanical methods, without the prior written permission of the publisher. For permission requests, contact Frederick Barnes +6422-634-7815. This is a work of non-fiction. All names, characters, and incidents portrayed in this book are real. Actual persons (living or deceased), places, buildings, and products are accurately depicted or referenced. Any similarities to fictional works are purely coincidental.

THE HEI-TIKI'S JOURNEY

TABLE OF CONTENTS
THE HEI-TIKI'S JOURNEY 2
    A True Story from Aotearoa New Zealand 3
PART ONE: THE GIFTING 3
PART TWO: THE SINKING 5
PART THREE: THE JOURNEY 11
PART FOUR: THE FINDING 14
PART FIVE: THE SEPARATION 19
PART SIX: THE RECOGNITION 23
PART EIGHT: THE CONFIRMATION 30
  EPILOGUE: THE NEW STORY 35
  AUTHOR'S NOTE 38

A True Story from Aotearoa New Zealand

PART ONE: THE GIFTING

On Fred's eighteenth birthday, beneath the wide Northland sky, his friend Rapine, who everyone called Pa, placed something precious into his hands.

"Hold it," Pa said, his dark eyes serious. "Feel its weight."

Fred closed his fingers around the greenstone. It was surprisingly heavy for its size, as if the stone held more than just rock inside it. The carving was a Hei-Tiki, a traditional guardian figure, smoothed and shaped by Pa's own hands during their final year at Whangaroa College.

"I made only a handful of these this year," Pa explained, watching Fred's face. "But this one... this one was different. When I was carving it, I could feel something in the stone. Mana. Power. Like it was already alive, just waiting to be freed."

Fred turned the greenstone over in his palm. The Hei-Tiki's tilted head seemed to look back at him with knowing eyes.

Its compact body, no bigger than his palm. It felt dense and solid. Heavier than any stone that size should be.

"It's a guardian," Pa said, fastening the braided cord around Fred's neck. "A kaitiaki. It'll watch over you."

Fred felt the Hei-Tiki settle against his chest, its weight both physical and something else. Something he couldn't quite name.

"Thank you, Pa," he said. "I'll take care of it."

"Nah, bro," Pa smiled. "It'll take care of you."

Among the friends gathered for the celebration was a girl named Myra, who would remember this moment years later when it mattered most. She watched Pa perform the small blessing, heard him speak about the stone's journey from Te Wai Pounamu, the South Island, to the Far North, and saw how carefully Fred touched the taonga, as if he understood its value even then.

For eleven years, the Hei-Tiki never left Fred's neck.

PART TWO: THE SINKING

By 2019, Fred had become a landscaper with his own company, Wicked Landscape Designs and Myra had become his partner in both life and their shared passion for protecting Northland's wild places. They rented a little place at Ota Point in Whangaroa Harbour, right beneath the ancient volcanic plug called Ohakiri, though most people knew it as St. Paul's Rock.

The property came with kayaks, which suited them perfectly. The harbour was one of their favorite places, one of the deepest harbours in the Southern Hemisphere, so deep that the Queen Mary herself had moored there once. The water held secrets and stories, sunken histories and hidden depths.

Labour Weekend arrived with the kind of golden autumn light that makes everything feel both urgent and eternal. Fred had spent months transforming the property's gardens, and now it was listed for sale. Everything was packed into boxes. The house stood empty.

"One last paddle?" Myra suggested, looking out at the glassy harbour.

"Definitely," Fred agreed, reaching for his life jacket. "The Hei-Tiki tour."

The name made them both smile. The greenstone had been with Fred through so many landscaping jobs where he worked until his hands bled, volunteer nights restoring native bush, proposals and promises and plans. It had rested against his heart for so long that he sometimes forgot it was there.

Until he didn't feel it anymore.

They were paddling around Peach Island/Ohauroro, when it happened.

Mid-stroke, Fred felt the cord snap.

One moment: the familiar weight against his chest, the slight pull of the leather as he leaned forward into the paddle stroke.

Next moment: nothing. A lightness that felt wrong. An absence that echoed louder than any presence ever had.

His heart dropped before his brain caught up.

"No," he whispered. Then louder: "NO!"

He stopped paddling so abruptly that his kayak rocked. His hands flew to his chest, searching for what he already knew was gone. The broken cord dangled uselessly around his neck, its frayed end telling a story that had no happy ending.

"What's wrong?" Myra called, pulling her kayak alongside his.

"The Hei-Tiki," Fred said, his voice hollow. "It broke. It's gone."

They both looked down into the water. The harbour here was impossibly deep, twenty, thirty, maybe forty meters. The kind of depth where light gives up halfway down, where currents move in ways that don't make sense from the surface, where things disappear into darkness and don't come back.

Somewhere down there, among the remnants of World War Two, unexploded mines that had never been fully cleared, Fred's Hei-Tiki was sinking.

Down.

Down.

Down.

Until even the last rays of sunlight couldn't follow it anymore.

Fred wanted to dive. Wanted to take a huge breath and follow the greenstone into the depths, even though he knew it was impossible. Even though he knew that the moment it left his hand, it had chosen a different path.

"Maybe it washed up on shore," Myra said, but her voice held the same hopelessness that Fred felt.

They searched anyway. Paddled slowly around Peach Island, scanning the shoreline, checking every rocky outcrop and sandy beach. But Whangaroa Harbour is vast, with dozens of bays and inlets, cliffs and caves, secret places where the water keeps its treasures.

When they finally paddled back to Ota Point as the sun set, Fred's chest felt empty. Not just because the Hei-Tiki was gone, but because so was his heart. They'd sunk together into the cold depths, and only one of them had surfaced.

For years, Fred couldn't tell Pa what had happened.

How do you tell someone that you lost the precious thing they made with their own hands? How do you explain that you failed to protect something that was supposed to protect you?

Meanwhile, life continued its relentless current. Fred's oldest brother died. Then his father. An aunty. His grandma. Friends. The years between 2019 and 2024 felt like standing in a river of loss, watching people you love float past like leaves, unable to hold onto any of them.

Sometimes, in the darkest moments, Fred would reach for the Hei-Tiki that wasn't there anymore, and the absence would hit him all over again. Another loss. Another failure. Another piece of his heart at the bottom of the harbour.

Finally, one day, he couldn't carry the secret anymore.

He found Pa and told him everything. The paddle. The snap. The sinking. The years of silence.

"I'm so sorry," Fred said, his voice breaking. "I know I should have told you sooner. I just... I couldn't."

Pa was quiet for a long time, his expression unreadable. Then he placed a hand on Fred's shoulder.

"You know what I think?" Pa said. "If it's meant to return, it will find you."

"But…"

"Trust, bro. Trust the stone. Trust the ocean. Trust the journey." Pa smiled, but his eyes were serious. "That Hei-Tiki had mana when I carved it. That kind of power doesn't just disappear. It goes where it needs to go."

Fred wanted to believe him. But wanting and believing are different countries, and he wasn't sure he had a passport to hope anymore.

PART THREE: THE JOURNEY

Here's what the humans didn't see:

The Hei-Tiki sank through water that turned from green to blue to black. Spinning slowly as it fell, catching the last threads of sunlight before entering a darkness that had existed since the harbour was formed by ancient volcanoes.

It landed on the sandy bottom with the softest sound, a whisper that only the deepest fish could hear.

And there it rested.

For days? Weeks? Time moves differently at the bottom of the ocean, where there's no sun to mark hours and no tide to mark days. The Hei-Tiki lay among the silt and shells, the lost anchors and sunken stories, the mysteries that the harbour holds in its deepest heart.

But the stone remembered. Remembered hands that carved it. Remembered the warmth of a chest that it had guarded. Remembered promises made under a Northland sky.

And slowly, so slowly, it began to move.

Maybe dolphins found it and carried it in their wake, curious about this unusual stone. Maybe orcas, those ocean wolves, pushed it along during their hunting rounds through the harbour. Maybe the taniwha, the great guardian serpents of Māori legend, decided this small guardian deserved to go home.

Or maybe, just maybe, the ocean itself recognized that this stone belonged somewhere else, and the currents became hands, and the tides became feet, and the whole harbour conspired to return what had been lost.

The Hei-Tiki tumbled across the seafloor, over rocks and through kelp forests. It was buffeted by storms that churned the deep water. It was smoothed by sand that acted like liquid time, polishing away edges, revealing the stone's true nature.

It grew smoother.

And somehow, impossibly, it grew heavier. As if the ocean was adding its own weight to the stone's mana. As if every meter traveled was teaching the Hei-Tiki something new about endurance, about patience, about finding your way home when the world seems impossibly vast.

Months passed in the human world above.

Below, the Hei-Tiki continued its mysterious journey.

Back toward Ota Point. Back toward the place it had been lost. Back toward a reunion that nobody believed was possible.

PART FOUR: THE FINDING

Alan was a kaumātua, a respected elder, who loved walking the beaches around Ota Point with his mokopuna, his grandchildren and great-grandchildren. The little ones ran ahead, as children do, scrambling over rocks slick with sea spray, poking at tide pools, collecting treasures that adults had forgotten to notice.

"Koro! Koro!" they called. "Come look!"

But Alan had stopped, his feet suddenly unwilling to move forward. He stood on the sand, feeling something he hadn't felt in years. A pull. A presence. A certainty that something important was waiting just around the corner.

He followed his mokopuna slowly, his heart beating harder than the gentle walk warranted.

And there, among the rock oysters and puddles of trapped seawater, among the salt-encrusted Neptune's necklaces and broken shells and ordinary beach debris, lay something extraordinary.

A Hei-Tiki. Greenstone. Bathed in sand.

Alan bent down, his knees protesting with age and picked it up.

The moment his fingers closed around the stone, he understood why he'd felt its mana before he'd seen it. This was no ordinary carving. This was a guardian that had traveled far and suffered much and survived everything the ocean could throw at it.

The cord was frayed and crusted with salt. The stone itself was smoother than any greenstone Alan had ever touched, as if the ocean had spent months polishing it with infinite patience.

And it was heavy. So heavy.

Not the physical weight, though that was notable, but the spiritual weight. The feeling that this small stone carried stories that would take a lifetime to tell.

"Taonga," Alan whispered, and his mokopuna gathered around to see what their koro had found.

Alan knew enough about tikanga, proper cultural protocols, to understand that finding a Māori taonga required guidance. He took the Hei-Tiki to a local minister named Kevin, a man who understood both the Christian faith and the deeper Māori traditions that ran like roots beneath this land. The Whangaroa locals knew Kevin by another name, "Kiwi".

"What should I do?" Alan asked, holding out the greenstone. "What's the right way to honor this finding?"

Kiwi examined the Hei-Tiki carefully, feeling its unusual weight, noting its incredible smoothness. Then he looked out the window toward Ota Point, where new neighbors were moving furniture into a house that had recently been sold.

"You found it at the edge of te moana," Kiwi said thoughtfully. "At the boundary between land and water, which is itself a sacred space. In the old traditions, that means the ocean has chosen you to be its next guardian."

"You're sure?" Alan asked.

"I'm sure that it found you for a reason," Kiwi replied. "Wear it with respect. Honor its mana. And trust that if it needs to travel again, it will make that clear too."

So Alan accepted the Hei-Tiki as a gift from the ocean.

He had the cord replaced, adjusted to fit his own frame. He wore it religiously, feeling its weight against his chest like a second heartbeat. And over the next few years, Alan and the Hei-Tiki traveled together.

Across oceans to visit family in distant countries. Through airports and hotels, beaches and mountains. The Hei-Tiki saw more of the world than it had in all its previous years.

When Alan fell ill and spent extended time in hospital, he swore the stone gave him strength. He would hold it during painful procedures, feeling its coolness against his palm, its weight anchoring him to life when his body wanted to drift away.

"You're protecting me," he would whisper to it. "Just like you protected whoever owned you before."

The Hei-Tiki's only response was its silent, steady presence. But sometimes, that's the most powerful answer of all.

PART FIVE: THE SEPARATION

Then, as mysteriously as it had appeared, the Hei-Tiki vanished again.

Alan couldn't explain it. He'd been staying at Kauri Lodge, a rest home in Whangaroa where he sometimes visited or stayed when he needed extra care. One day the greenstone was around his neck. The next day, it wasn't.

He searched frantically. Tore through his belongings. Asked every staff member. Offered rewards for its safe return.

"It's a family heirloom," he told everyone, which wasn't quite true but felt true. The Hei-Tiki had become his family. "Please, if anyone finds a greenstone necklace, it's incredibly important to me."

Days passed. Then weeks. Then months.

The Hei-Tiki didn't reappear.

Alan's hope began to fade, the way hope does when loss becomes familiar. He'd carried the stone for years, felt its protection, trusted in its mana. And now it was gone, and he didn't even know how to begin mourning something so small yet so significant.

He eventually stopped searching. Stopped asking. Stopped offering rewards.

The Hei-Tiki was gone. That was that.

Or so he thought.

What Alan didn't know was that an old woman at Kauri Lodge had found the greenstone.

She had dementia, this elderly lady, and spent her days wandering the halls of the rest home, collecting treasures that spoke to her in ways she couldn't quite articulate. She had several kete, traditional woven bags, that she filled with her findings, stashing them in various hiding places throughout the facility.

One day, she felt something calling to her.

"It's here," she muttered, shuffling through corridors. "It's calling. Can you hear it?"

The nurses smiled kindly, used to her wandering and her conversations with invisible presences. But the old woman was insistent. She stopped outside a room, cocked her head like a bird listening for worms, then shuffled inside with surprising purpose.

There, on the floor where it had somehow fallen, lay the Hei-Tiki.

The old woman picked it up with reverent hands. Despite the fog in her mind, or perhaps because of it, she recognized what she held.

"Kaitiaki," she whispered. "Guardian. Taonga. So much mana."

She carried it carefully to one of her kete, where it joined other treasures: buttons and bottle caps, smooth stones and shiny wrappers and jewels that looked the same to her clouded eyes.

The kete was stored in a dark cupboard near the dementia unit, where time moved slowly and memories dissolved like sugar in rain.

And there the Hei-Tiki waited. Again.

Patient as stone. Steady as the ocean. Knowing that journeys have their own timing, and some things can't be rushed.

PART SIX: THE RECOGNITION

Myra walked into the office at Kauri Lodge to drop off some paperwork to the Kauri Lodge reception desk.

A greenstone Hei-Tiki, hanging on a hook in the duty room.

She stopped mid-sentence, her brain struggling to process what her eyes were seeing.

"Where... where did that come from?" she asked, pointing.

"Oh, we found it in one of the residents' kete," the staff member explained. "One of our ladies with dementia had been collecting things. We rescued it from the cupboard and hung it here, hoping someone would claim it. We think it belongs to Alan, he was looking for a greenstone necklace a while back, we've called him, Allen will be coming in any day now for that precious green stone Hei-tiki of his."

Myra moved closer, her heart starting to pound.

The carving style. The size. The particular tilt of the head. The way the stone seemed to carry weight that had nothing to do with gravity.

"Can I... can I hold it?" she asked.

The staff member took it down and placed it in Myra's hands.

The moment her fingers closed around the greenstone, she knew. She absolutely knew.

"I think..." Myra's voice shook. "I think I know who this belongs to. I was there when it was first gifted. I watched Pa, Rapine, give this to Fred at his eighteenth birthday. I remember the blessing."

"But how would it get here?" the staff member asked, confused.

"That," Myra said, staring at the Hei-Tiki with wonder, "is a very long story."

The pieces came together slowly, like a puzzle reassembling itself:

Alan had found it at Ota Point, the exact place Fred and Myra had been living when the Hei-Tiki was lost. The new neighbors Kevin, Kiwi mentioned? That had been around the same time Fred and Myra moved out, their kayaking days at Ota Point ending.

The old woman saying it "called to her"? That it was a guardian? She'd been right. More right than anyone could have explained.

The smoothness Alan mentioned? That was the ocean's work, polishing the stone during its months-long journey across the harbour floor.

The unusual weight? Pa had felt that when he first carved it. The mana that made this Hei-Tiki different from all the others.

Every piece fitted. Every mystery had an answer.

The Hei-Tiki had traveled in a great circle. Lost at Ota Point. Found at Ota Point. Carried across oceans and through hospitals. Hidden in a kete by a woman whose confused mind somehow recognized its power. And finally, recognized by someone who'd been there at the beginning.

"We need to contact Alan," Myra said. "And Fred. They need to meet."

PART SEVEN: THE RETURN

The meeting was arranged for a sunny afternoon at Kauri Lodge. Alan arrived with a mixture of curiosity and confusion, he still didn't understand how a greenstone could possibly belong to this young landscaper he'd never met before.

Fred arrived with his heart in his throat and hardly dared to hope.

When Alan handed him the Hei-Tiki, Fred's hands shook so badly he almost dropped it.

But the moment the stone settled into his palm, he knew. The weight. The smoothness. The way it seemed to pulse with recognition, as if it too was saying: I'm home. Finally, I'm home.

"It's mine," Fred whispered. "It's really mine."

"But how?" Alan asked. "I found it at Ota Point years ago."

So Fred told the story. All of it. Pa's carving and the eighteenth birthday blessing. The eleven years of wearing it constantly. The kayak trip and the broken cord and the sinking, down into Whangaroa Harbour's impossible depths.

The years of grief, the Hei-Tiki lost, and so many people lost too, his brother and father and aunty and grandmother, loss upon loss upon loss.

The guilt of not telling Pa. And Pa's wisdom: If it's meant to return, it will find you.

Alan listened with growing wonder. When Fred finished, the elder was quiet for a long moment.

"I didn't find it randomly," Alan said slowly. "I felt it before I saw it. Felt its mana pulling me toward that beach. And all these years I wore it, through all my travels, through my hospital stays when I needed strength... I was just its guardian for a while. Keeping it safe until it could come home."

"You gave it back its story," Fred said. "You gave it adventures it never would have had. You carried it when I couldn't."

"And that lady with dementia," Myra added softly. "She recognized what it was, called it kaitiaki, taonga. Even with her memory fading, she knew."

They all sat with that truth for a moment. The Hei-Tiki had been protected every step of its journey, by ocean currents that carried it home, by an elder who felt its mana, by a confused woman who saw clearly what others might miss, by nurses who rescued it from darkness, by Myra who recognized it.

It had never been lost. It had been traveling.

"I have something for you," Fred said, pulling out a carefully wrapped package, Pa helped me find this one. "It was also blessed by Mary Smith, a respected Kuia elder for the Matangirau Te Towai Marae earlier this morning. It's not a replacement, nothing could replace your time with the Hei-Tiki, but it's an exchange. A thank you. A completion of the circle."

He unwrapped a beautiful fishing hook carved from Northland greenstone, newly blessed, ready to begin its own journey.

Alan took it with reverent hands. "This is proper tikanga," he said softly. "The exchange of taonga. Both stones continuing their own way on separate journeys."

They took a photo together, Fred and Alan, both wearing their greenstone carvings visible. A moment of history. A story that defied logic but demanded to be believed because it was true.

Before they parted, Alan placed his hand on Fred's shoulder.

"Take care of it," he said. "But not too carefully. Let it live. Let it have adventures. And if it leaves you again..." He smiled. "Trust the journey."

PART EIGHT: THE CONFIRMATION

Fred needed one more thing before he could fully believe. One more confirmation that this impossible story was real and to prove the Hei-tiki had physically returned at long last.

He found Pa in Kerikeri, shopping in the township's small center. It wasn't planned, just one of those moments when the universe arranges meetings that need to happen.

"Pa!" Fred called out. "Wait! I need to show you something."

Rapine turned, saw Fred's face, and knew immediately that something significant had happened.

Fred held out the Hei-Tiki without saying a word.

Pa took it. Weighed it in his palm. Ran his thumb over its impossibly smooth surface. Turned it over to examine the carving details he'd created with his own hands nearly two decades ago.

For a long moment, he said nothing.

Then: "It's real. It's the one I made."

"You're sure?" Fred asked, even though he already knew.

"Feel this," Pa said, pressing the stone into Fred's hand. "That weight? I felt that when I was carving it. Told you about it at your eighteenth. This stone has always been heavier than it should be. Denser. Like it's carrying something extra."

He ran his fingers over the surface again. "And this smoothness... I didn't make it this smooth. This is ocean work. Months of sand and current, polishing it. Making it even more perfect than when it left my hands."

Pa looked at Fred with eyes that had seen a lot of life but had rarely seen something this miraculous.

"I told you," Pa said quietly. "If it's meant to return, it will find you. The Hei-Tiki chose to come home."

"But why?" Fred asked. "Why go through all that? Why not just stay lost, or stay with Alan? Why fight so hard to come back?"

Pa smiled. "Because it's not done with you yet. It's your kaitiaki, bro. Your guardian. And guardians don't abandon their people just because the journey gets hard."

He handed the Hei-Tiki back with ceremony, the way he'd first given it eighteen years before.

"You lost it during hard years," Pa said. "When your brother died. Your dad. Your grandma. So many people are leaving. Maybe the Hei-Tiki needed to leave too, for a while. Travel. Learn. Get stronger." He tapped the stone gently. "And then come back when you are ready to receive it again. When you could see it not as something you failed to protect, but as something that chose you."

Fred's eyes softened slightly although still firm and serious. "I thought I'd failed you. Failed the stone."

"Nah," Pa said. "You learned. That's different. You learned that some things leave so they can teach you how to let go. And some things return so they can teach you how to hold on."

The End.

EPILOGUE: THE NEW STORY

Fred wears the Hei-Tiki again now, the cord replaced and adjusted, the stone resting against his chest like it never left.

But it's different this time.

Before, it was a gift from a friend. Precious, yes. Important, absolutely. But still just an object, however beautiful and powerful.

Now it's a story. A journey. A testament to impossible returns and mysterious guardians and the way things find their way home when the time is right.

Now when Fred touches the Hei-Tiki, he feels:

The moment Pa carved it, sensing something special in the stone.

The blessing at his eighteenth birthday, Myra watching and remembering.

The eleven years of carrying it through work and love and ordinary days.

The snap of the cord, the sinking, the years of loss and grief.

The ocean's patient hands, polishing and protecting and carrying it home.

Alan, finding the Hei-tiki. Feeling its mana, giving it adventures across multiple oceans.

The old woman's confused clarity: "It's calling. It's a guardian."

Myra's recognition and the circle closing.

Pa's confirmation: "You learned to let go. Now learn to hold on."

All of it lives in the stone now. All of it has added weight to its mana.

Fred knows the Hei-Tiki might leave again someday. Cords break. Stories demand new chapters. Guardians sometimes need to guard other people for a while.

But he's not afraid of that anymore.

Because he's learned what Pa always knew: some things are meant to return. Some journeys are circles. And some guardians protect you even when you can't see them, even when you think they're lost forever.

The Hei-Tiki rests against Fred's chest, smooth and heavy and impossibly home.

And if you listen very carefully, if you put your ear close to the greenstone and hold very, very still, you might hear it still carrying the sound of the ocean.

The sound of a journey that was never about being lost. Only about finding the way home.

AUTHOR'S NOTE

This story is true. All of it.

Fred (that's me, I'm telling you my own story) I really did lose the Hei-Tiki in Whangaroa Harbour in 2019. Really did spend years unable to tell Pa what happened. Nearly did give up hope of ever seeing it again.

Alan really did find it at Ota Point, at the exact location where I'd been living when it sank. Really did wear it for years, travel with it, feel it protect him through illness.

The old woman with dementia really did say it "called to her" and recognized it as a guardian.

Myra really did see it hanging in the Kauri Lodge office and recognized it from my eighteenth birthday party.

Pa really did hold it in Kerikeri and confirm it was the genuine article, smoother and still impossibly heavy.

And the exchange ceremony with Alan really happened, blessed, proper and right.

I'm still finding pieces of sand packed into the carved corners. Still marveling at its smoothness. Still feeling its weight and wondering how a stone can survive months at the bottom of one of the deepest harbours in the Southern Hemisphere and come back more perfect than before.

The only part I can't tell you for certain, is the Hei-Tiki's underwater journey. I don't know if dolphins carried it, or orcas, or taniwha, or just the ocean's patient currents.

But I know this: it came home.

And sometimes, that's the only miracle we need to believe in.

Additional Notes:

Kevin, whom we called Kiwi, was more than a neighbor, he was a dear friend of my father's and served as minister for both my brother Curtis's and father's funeral services. Mary Smith, a respected Kuia, also officiated alongside Kiwi at my father's Funeral.

My father dedicated much of his life to Landcare conservation work, protecting New Zealand's native wildlife, flora and fauna, with particular devotion to one of our national icons: the kiwi bird. Curtis was a passionate fisherman and explorer who spent countless hours scaling the foreshores and discovering the hidden reaches of

Whangaroa Harbour and our local coastline, he knew these waters intimately.

My brother Mark and our shared mum have also explored much of this area and the coastlines and deep water beyond with me. During various Kayaking, hiking and camping expeditions on various islands with the owners prior permission.

Since that eighteenth birthday when he first gifted me the Hei-Tiki, Pa has achieved remarkable things. He's ridden and paddled in traditional waka, participated in countless ceremonies, and earned recognition in the Paihia Museum with a large photographic display showing him in traditional clothing alongside his crew. He's become a master weaver, creating exquisite hats/potae and cloaks adorned with kiwi feathers and other culturally significant bird plumage, all while continuing his carving and other traditional crafts.

Myra has developed deep expertise in producing high-grade traditional Māori Rongoa, healing balms, lotions and a comprehensive range of therapeutic products.

Her dedication to higher university grade study has not only gained her invaluable knowledge, it has also earned her numerous qualifications, including business and property management and certificates in traditional healing arts.

Not to mention the positive effects, she has given heaps, received plenty of interest from the general public, friends and family. Many of which have been healed or healing from natural medicines produced locally and distributed to them fresh in the process.

As for me, I've continued my restorative conservation work and published a few books, with many more in various stages of drafting. My hands have learned many trades: timber working and sculpting and panel beating to mention but a few. With skills in mechanical repairs, high quality paint jobs.

I once worked at the largest foundry in the Southern Hemisphere, the place was owned by Bradkens and its facility was located in Runcorn, Australia.

This is where I became proficient in welding, mold making, and industrial assembly. I spent some time living off-grid with New Zealand Māori and Australian Aboriginal communities.

Each of us has continued walking our own paths, carrying lessons from taonga like the Hei-Tiki. They should teach or remind us about journeys, returns. The connections that bind us to each other and to this land.

Glossary of Māori Terms:

Hei-Tiki - Traditional Māori neck pendant, usually carved from greenstone
Pounamu - Greenstone/jade, highly valued in Māori culture
Kaitiaki - Guardian, protector
Taonga - Treasure, something precious
Mana - Prestige, spiritual power, authority
Tikanga - Correct procedure, customs, protocols
Kaumātua - Elder, respected older person
Mokopuna - Grandchildren, descendants
Te Moana - The ocean
Kete - Woven flax basket
Pa - Fortified village (also used as nickname in this story)
Taniwha - Powerful supernatural beings in Māori tradition
Koro - Grandfather (term of respect for elders)

<u>Final acknowledgments</u>

To my old friend Pa, for always being there for me. Amongst many things he has taught me that some things return when they're ready.

For Alan, my new friend, who kept the Hei-tiki warm and gave it an extended family/whanau and took it everywhere with him so the Hei-tiki could experience a broader life and travel a larger portion of earth's surface, passing over and beyond the horizon many times.

For Myra, my loyally devoted partner, who also recognized what others might have missed.

For the Hei-Tiki, for your guidance, persistence and for finding your way back to me, I will remember you always. If you choose to depart on another epic whirlwind adventure, I will not lose hope, for you too remember, and long for home.

www.ingramcontent.com/pod-product-compliance
Lightning Source LLC
Chambersburg PA
CBHW051426070526
44584CB00023B/3598